A Joshua Morris Book
Published by The Reader's Digest Association, Inc.
Copyright © 1993 Victoria House Ltd.
All rights reserved. Unauthorized reproduction,
in any manner, is prohibited.
Printed in Hong Kong.
Library of Congress Catalog Number: 92-62551
ISBN: 0-89577-482-8
10 9 8 7 6 5 4 3 2 1

WETLANDS

NATURE SEARCH

Author
ANDREW LANGLEY

Consultant
PROF. JOSEPH S. LARSON

Illustrators
NEIL BULPITT   DAVID HOLMES
BRIN EDWARDS   EVA MELHUISH

a Joshua Morris book
from The Reader's Digest Association, Inc.

CONTENTS

How It Works	7
Desert Delta	8
Peat Bog Nursery	10
Freshwater Forest	12
Tundra Maze	14
Spot the Difference	16
Mysterious Salt Marsh	18
Muddy Mangrove	20
Puzzle Answers	22
Glossary	26

HOW IT WORKS

WETLANDS

Swamps, bogs, and marshes are different types of wetlands. They are home to a great variety of animals and plants. Here you can explore these wetlands and discover the exciting and colorful wildlife that live here. Some are hidden or camouflaged — use your magnifying glass to search these wet places and see what you can find.

The magnifying glass  on each page indicates the creatures you should look for.

There are other challenges to test your powers of observation. For instance, somewhere you'll find a tiger who is missing some stripes.

There is a glossary at the back of the book where you can find out about the creatures that appear on every page.

DESERT DELTA

The Okavango, in southern Africa, is a river that never reaches the sea. Instead, it flows into the desert and disappears in the parched sand and rock. But at the desert's edge the river fans out into a huge delta of swamps, lagoons, and small islands. This delta is home for an amazing variety of plants and animals.

Bright water lilies cover open stretches of water, and thick clumps of papyrus and reeds choke the channels. In places the reeds are so tall and thick that it is hard to find a way through, and only birds can come and go easily. Many feed on clouds of mayflies and midges. Others, like the malachite kingfisher, the fish eagle, and the reed cormorant, snatch fish from the water. Swamp snakes, boomslangs, and other reptiles slither among the plant stems in search of food. The hippopotamus, however, is so big and heavy that it can force a path through the thickest reed clumps.

THE CATFISH RUN

Each year, when the river is low, big shoals of catfish make wild ''runs'' upstream. They thrash the reed stems and churn the water, scaring smaller fish out of hiding and snapping them up. On the lookout for an easy meal, birds and snakes follow the catfish.

CAN YOU FIND THEM?

Many small creatures live among the papyrus and reeds of the delta swamps. Using your magnifying glass, can you find the following in the picture?

The Pel's fishing owl hunts at night. Its hooting can be heard almost 2 miles away.

Flap-necked chameleons live in motsaudi trees. They match the shape and color of the leaves.

Blister beetles are attracted by the scent of the day lily and feed on its flowers.

Dragonflies hover over the swamp water, catching midges and other tiny insects out of the air.

The fishing spider hooks itself to a reed with its back legs and catches fish with its front legs.

The swamp rat has webbed feet, which make it a good swimmer and help it move easily through the reeds.

PEAT BOG NURSERY

The flat, still bogs of northern Europe spread out like a carpet of moss and grass. Here, what looks like solid ground can actually be as soft as jelly in places, filled with pools and water channels. Plants decay slowly in this water, but eventually they settle on the bottom and, over thousands of years, turn into peat.

Butterflies, grasshoppers, and craneflies fly between sedges and sundew plants. The stems provide good cover for the fox as it slinks after voles and other small mammals. The plaintive cries of the curlew, the sandpiper, and other wading birds echo across the landscape. There are five sandpipers flying overhead. Spot the two that are the same. There are also four small craneflies to find!

SPOT THE PARENT

Some babies look very different from their parents. These are the young of some of the animals in the main picture. Can you find the parent that each baby belongs to?

The caterpillar hatches from the eggs laid by the purple-edged copper butterfly. It will turn into a chrysalis before emerging as a young adult butterfly.

This tadpole is a baby newt. It must beware of danger from its enemies, which include dragonflies — and other tadpoles!

The crane chick is clumsy and weak. It waits in the nest for its parents to bring food.

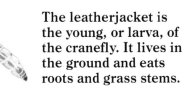

The leatherjacket is the young, or larva, of the cranefly. It lives in the ground and eats roots and grass stems.

Dragonfly nymphs live in the water. They can swim very fast by jetting out water behind them.

SUGAR SUCKERS

Butterflies can feed only by drinking. Their main source of food is nectar, a sugary liquid found in flowers. The butterfly sucks up the nectar through a long tube, like a flexible drinking straw. This tube, called the proboscis, lies beneath the butterfly's head. When it is not being used, the proboscis is neatly rolled up.

Proboscis

A FROG GROWS UP

A frog is an amphibian. This means that it spends part of its life in water and part on land. It starts out as an egg, floating in a jellylike mass in the water. The egg hatches into a tadpole, which swims about, slowly growing legs and lungs. After several weeks, its tail disappears and it comes out onto the land.

FRESHWATER FOREST

The Florida Everglades is a region of swampy woods and grasslands in the southern tip of Florida. Clumps of cypresses and other tall trees form islands in the swamps. They are swathed in smaller tropical plants, such as strangler figs, wildpines, and ferns. Under the trees it is dark and quiet. All that can be heard is the occasional splash of an alligator or the buzz of countless insects. The swamp water creeps slowly through the Everglades toward the sea. Although it is shallow, it teems with life, providing food for many kinds of animals. Limpkins and kites search for snails, and roseate spoonbills shovel up insects and crayfish. Garpike and turtles lurk in the water, ready to grab small fish and other animals.

PELICAN PARTY

White pelicans live — and hunt — together in large groups. They swim along in a line, driving the fish in front of them. When the fish reach shallow water, the pelicans scoop them up in their big pouched bills.

CAN YOU FIND THEM?

The dark and shady swamp is an ideal place to hide. Using your magnifying glass, see how many of the following creatures you can find.

The eastern coral snake is very brightly colored. It has poisonous fangs and eats lizards and other snakes.

The Florida panther is one of the rarest of all big cats. It hunts at night for deer and small mammals.

The opossum is a marsupial animal, whose tiny babies are nursed in the mother's pouch.

MANATEES

Manatees live in the deeper channels of the Everglades. They eat reeds and other water plants and dig down into the mud for roots. In this way, they help keep the swamp channels clear.

A manatee has to eat a lot. It can weigh as much as 2,200 pounds and may need more than 75 pounds of plant food a day to stay alive.

The green anole is a lizard with pads on its fingers and toes. These pads help it climb trees.

Tree snails eat the tiny fungi and other growths on the trunks of trees. They come in many different colors.

Muskrats use their scaly tails to swim and steer in the water. They live in burrows or make houses from reeds and grass.

13

TUNDRA MAZE

In winter, the Arctic tundra is a harsh place. There is no sun for many months, and icy winds blast across the frozen, snow-covered ground.

But during the short summer, the sun appears, melting the snow and thawing a thin layer of soil. About three feet down, the ground is still frozen, so the water cannot drain away and instead forms pools and bogs.

The light and warmth bring the tundra to life for a few short weeks. Plants hurry to put out their flowers, and the air is filled with clouds of newly hatched mosquitos and blackflies. Lemmings and ptarmigans eat the fresh green shoots, and wading birds search out insects and larvae. Caribou migrate north to feed on leaves and lichens. They must all be wary of the tundra predators, such as wolverines, foxes, and snowy owls.

There are six antlers hidden in the picture. Can you find them?

LOST LEMMING

This lemming wants to reach his friend in his burrow. But he must keep out of the water. Can you find a route for him to take so that he moves only on land?

WINTER COATS

The Arctic fox, the short-tailed weasel, and the ptarmigan have a white coat in winter. This makes them hard to see in the snow. In summer, when the snow melts, they lose their thick white coats and turn brown.

Arctic fox

Short-tailed weasel

Ptarmigan

SPOT THE DIFFERENCE

The lush grasses and fresh water of the Assam marshlands in India attract wildlife of all kinds. Some animals live here all year round. Others come just to feed or, during the spring, to breed.

The marshes make a perfect refuge for the pheasant-tailed jacana. When danger threatens, the young jacanas dive into the water and hide beneath the lily leaves. The noisy hill mynah is safe up in the trees, where it feeds on fruit and insects.

Also perched high in the trees is the Pallas's fish-eagle, ready to swoop down and snatch fish in its talons. The Indian darter swims below the water in search of fish and then holds up its wings to dry.

Barasingha and gaur come to drink and graze at the water's edge. They are always on the alert for hungry tigers on the prowl.

Large mammals also enjoy the water plants and grasses of the marshes. The Indian elephant tears off leaves and shoots with its long trunk, while the one-horned rhinoceros plunges into the water to find juicier shrubs. On the backs of these giants, cattle egrets search for insects and skin grubs. And where their huge feet have stirred up the mud, the birds snap up insects and small lizards.

There are ten differences between the picture on the right and the one on the left. Can you find all of them? And if you look carefully, you will find six tiger butterflies.

17

MYSTERIOUS SALT MARSH

The salt marshes on the East Coast of North America are formed by rivers on their way to the sea. A river slows down, and the sand and mud it is carrying sinks to the bottom, where it settles and gradually builds up into banks. Soon tough plants begin to grow, and more mud is caught in their stems. The banks grow higher, and more plants spring up. The marsh quickly attracts animals. Shore birds, like the clapper rail, nest among the stems, and rabbits and geese feed on the grasses. Gliding above the salt marsh, owls and harriers hunt for shrews and voles below. The nearby sea is a rich hunting ground for fish-eating birds, including the red-breasted merganser and the glossy ibis.

SHREW CARAVANS

Shrews raise their young in nests until they are old enough to venture out.

Some baby shrews explore the outside world in "caravans." Led by the mother, they form a line, each holding tight to the one in front with its teeth.

CAN YOU FIND THEM?

Several small creatures live among the tall plant stems of the salt-marsh grasses, where they are hidden from predators. Can you find them with your magnifying glass?

The raccoon eats almost anything, from fish and crabs to berries, grasshoppers, and mice.

Short-horned grasshoppers can jump a distance twenty times the length of their own bodies.

The marsh periwinkle shelters among the cordgrass, waiting for the gentle tide to bring food.

MIGRANT VISITORS

Willets and several other wading birds spend the winter in South America and fly north for the summer. They are known as "migrants." On the way, they stop off to feed in the coastal salt marshes. They catch fish and shellfish, and some dig up the buried eggs of the horseshoe crab.

The belted kingfisher hovers over the water before diving for fish. It also eats insects and small frogs.

A female mosquito feeds on the blood of a mammal by stabbing it with her sharp proboscis.

The marsh rice rat is a good swimmer and hunts the water's edge for snails and shellfish.

MUDDY MANGROVE

As the tide goes out in the Australian mangrove swamp, an eerie world is uncovered. The glistening mud clicks and pops as shellfish begin to stir. Just above, a vast tangle of thick roots drips with sea water. These are the long roots of the mangrove, one of the few plants that can live in the thick mud and salt water. It absorbs the water but gets rid of the salt, and its shallow roots spread out wide to give it strong support. Mud and other debris are caught in the roots, providing homes and food for many kinds of small creatures.

At low tide, fiddler crabs and mudskippers move across the mudflats looking for tiny plants and animals. The Radjah shelduck, comb-crested jacana, and brolga dig up shellfish and roots with their bills. When the tide comes in, the mudskippers climb up the mangrove roots and the crabs retreat to their holes.

There are four fiddler crabs in the picture. Can you find them all?

CAN YOU FIND THEM?

The tangle of mangrove roots and branches makes a fine hiding place. Can you find these creatures with your magnifying glass?

The longhorn beetle has antennae that are often longer than the rest of its body.

The brahminy kite hunts close to the ground, then swoops down to catch frogs, small reptiles, insects, and fish.

Weaver ants build their nests from mangrove and other leaves. They curl the leaves over and stick the edges together.

The lilac-crowned wren eats insects, earthworms, spiders, small crabs, and seeds.

A male cicada makes a loud buzzing noise by vibrating pieces of the shell on the underside of its body.

The carpet python coils around its eggs after they are laid. It stays with the eggs until they are hatched.

CROCODILE CRECHE

Saltwater crocodiles are very careful mothers. They bury their eggs and guard them closely. When the eggs are ready to hatch, the mother digs them out and helps the babies out of the shells. Then she gently picks up the babies in her mouth and carries them to the water.

PUZZLE ANSWERS

Marshes, swamps, and bogs are some of the richest and most exciting wildlife areas in the world. They are called "wetlands" and can be found almost anywhere, from the Atlantic Coast to the Indian hills, and from the frozen North to the torrid African desert.

There are three main types of wetlands, each one home to a great variety of plants and animals. Marshes are low-lying places that are regularly flooded by rivers or seawater. Swamps are flooded all the time and are thickly covered with plants such as reeds or trees. Bogs are soft, flat areas where the water cannot drain away.

Today, many wetland areas are in danger. They are being drained and turned into farmland. However, scientists now realize the great importance of these damp places and have begun to study them more closely. Several big wetlands have become major nature reserves.

Now that you have tried to find the animals with your magnifying glass, you can check the positions. In the following pictures, each position is shown by a circle.

Answers to questions are listed with the pictures.

DESERT DELTA

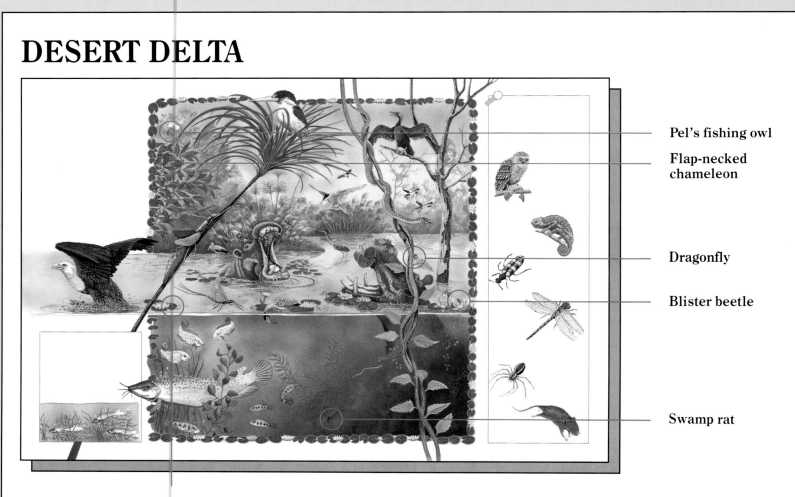

Pel's fishing owl

Flap-necked chameleon

Dragonfly

Blister beetle

Swamp rat

Fishing spider

PEAT BOG NURSERY

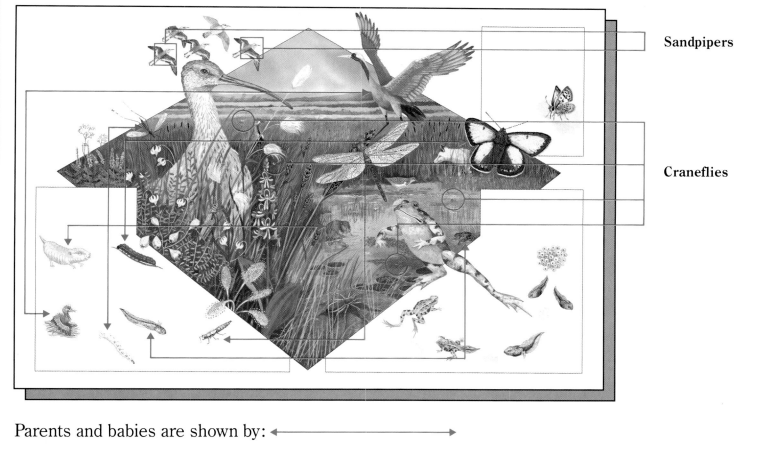

Sandpipers

Craneflies

Parents and babies are shown by: ⟵―――――――⟶

FRESHWATER FOREST

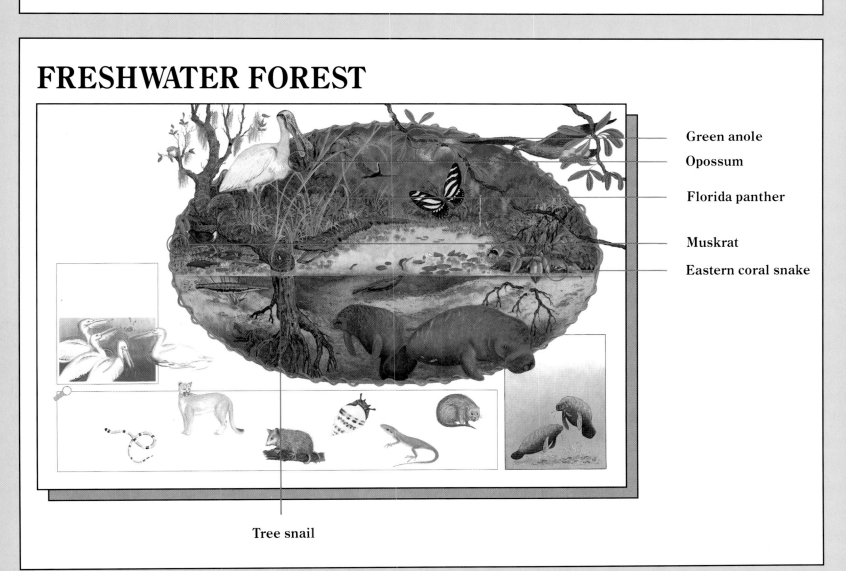

Green anole

Opossum

Florida panther

Muskrat

Eastern coral snake

Tree snail

TUNDRA MAZE

Antlers

This is the route the lemming should take.

SPOT THE DIFFERENCE

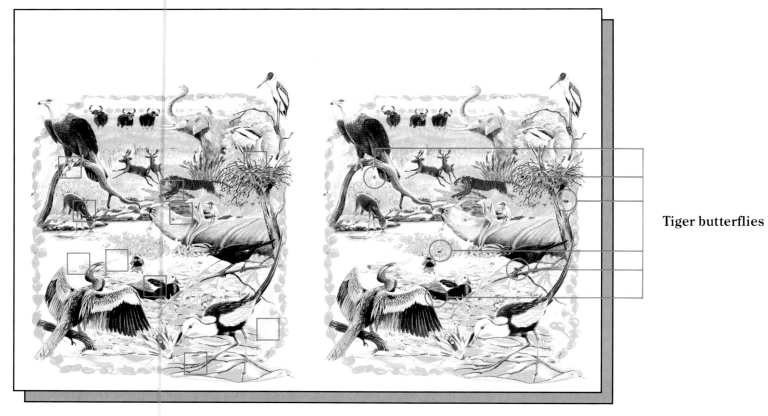

Tiger butterflies

The differences are shown by: ☐

MYSTERIOUS SALT MARSH

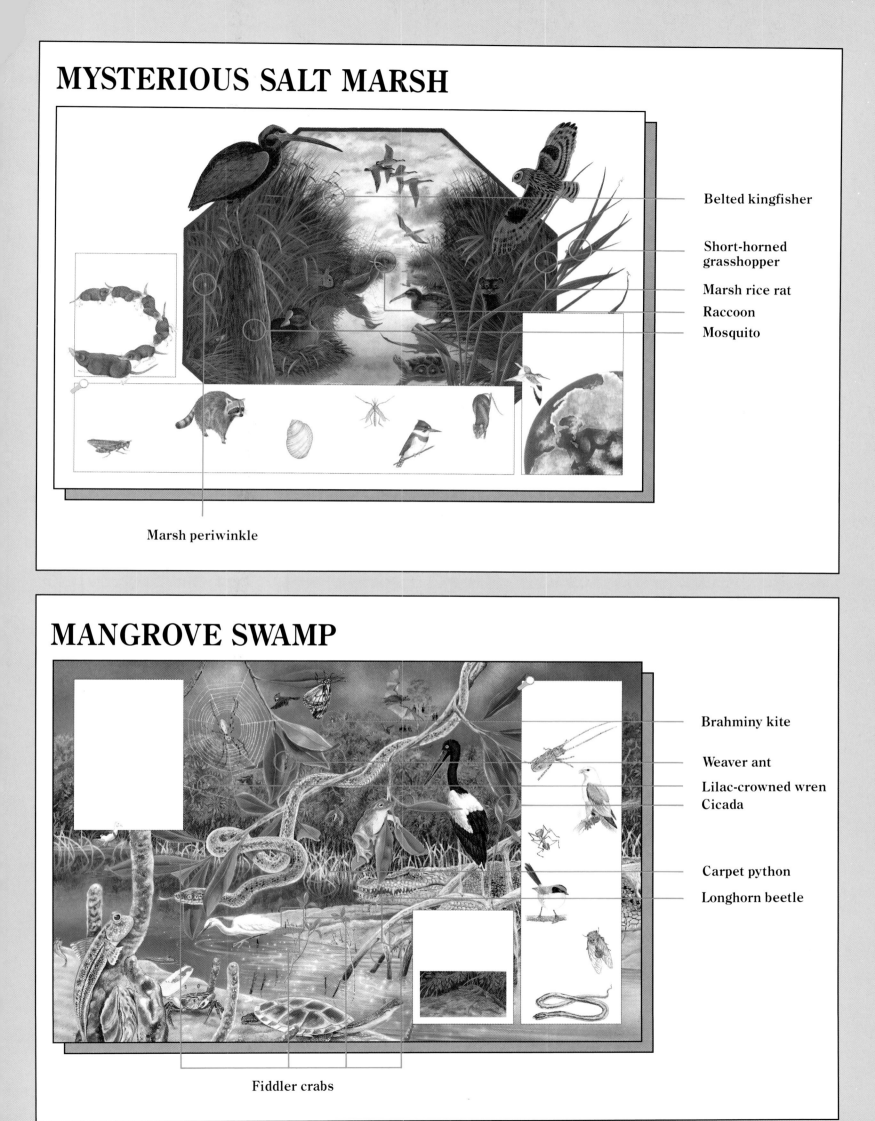

Belted kingfisher

Short-horned grasshopper

Marsh rice rat

Raccoon

Mosquito

Marsh periwinkle

MANGROVE SWAMP

Brahminy kite

Weaver ant

Lilac-crowned wren
Cicada

Carpet python

Longhorn beetle

Fiddler crabs

GLOSSARY

DESERT DELTA
pages 8–9

 African fish eagle
The fish eagle soars over the lagoons, searching for fish to catch in its strong talons.

Blister beetle
The blister beetle has a substance in its blood that causes blisters if it is rubbed on bare skin.

Boomslang
The boomslang is a poisonous green snake that steals eggs and young birds from their nests.

Dragonfly
The dragonfly has enormous eyes that cover most of the head and can look in any direction.

 Dwarf mouthbrooder
The male mouthbrooder attracts a mate by shimmering his body. The female carries her eggs in her mouth.

Fishing spider
The fishing spider can catch fish up to twice its own size.

 Flap-necked chameleon
Like other chameleons, this creature catches insects with its long sticky tongue.

Giant stick insect
Stick insects look just like the twigs they live on. They feed on the leaves and flowers of the knobthorn tree.

 **Hippopotamus**
The hippopotamus keeps cool in the water by day and comes out to feed on island plants at night.

Jewel cichlid
Jewel cichlids breed among the stems of lilies and reeds. Both parent fish take care of the young as they grow.

Malachite kingfisher
Many malachite kingfishers make their nests in termite mounds. They fly low over the water hunting for fish.

Mayfly
Adult mayflies die 2 or 3 days after mating. The eggs develop into nymphs, which may take a year to become adults.

Painted reed frog
The skin of reed frogs is sensitive to light. In the heat of the midday sun, the skin turns almost white.

 Pel's fishing owl
The Pel's fishing owl often builds its nest in the fork of the mokutshumo tree. It lines the nest with chips of bark.

 Peter's epauletted fruit bat
This fruit bat feeds at night on sycamore figs. By day, it roosts in large groups in shady trees.

Purple heron
The purple heron has very long toes that help it walk over floating plants without sinking.

Pygmy goose
Pygmy geese dive beneath the water to find lily fruits, which they peck open for the seeds.

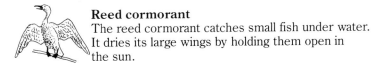 **Reed cormorant**
The reed cormorant catches small fish under water. It dries its large wings by holding them open in the sun.

 Saddle-billed stork
The saddle bill is Africa's largest stork. It flies to flooded areas to pick up the fish brought in by the waters.

 Sharp-toothed catfish
The sharp-toothed catfish grows up to 3 feet in length. It lives in the main channels of the delta.

 Striped swamp snake
The swamp snake is a fast swimmer. It rests with its head above water so that it can breathe.

 Swamp rat
Swamp rats live in burrows among the thick reeds and grasses on the banks of the lagoons.

 Whiskered tern
Whiskered terns swoop low over the water, feeding on the huge clouds of mayflies that emerge at night.

Yellow-billed stork
This large bird nests high up among the water fig trees that grow on small islands in the area.

PEAT BOG NURSERY
pages 10–11

 **Bank vole**
Bank voles have round muzzles, small ears, and short tails. They feed on grasses and sedges.

Crane
The crane is a tall bird that nests on the ground or over shallow water. It has a loud, trumpeting call.

 Cranefly
Craneflies have very long legs and thin bodies. Cranefly larvae are called leatherjackets.

Curlew
The curlew is a wading bird with a long, curved bill that it pokes into the soft mud in search of food.

 Dragonfly
Dragonflies can hover or even fly backwards; they are fierce hunters of other insects. Their larvae are called nymphs.

 European common frog
Common frogs spend the winter in mud and emerge in the spring to lay their eggs, or spawn. Baby frogs are called tadpoles.

 Golden plover
The golden plover is a wading bird with a short bill and pointed wings. It nests in a dip in open ground.

 Great crested newt
The male great crested newt grows a tall, crinkled crest along its back during the breeding season.

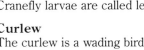 **Greenshank**
The greenshank gets its name from its green legs, or shanks. They trail behind it when it flies.

Marsh grasshopper
The male marsh grasshopper makes a soft ticking sound by tapping its front wings with its back legs.

Purple-edged copper butterfly
The purple-edged copper is a small, brightly colored butterfly. While it is still a caterpillar, it feeds on docks and knotgrasses.

Raft spider
The female raft spider lays her eggs in a small cocoon, which she carries with her until the young hatch.

Red fox
The red fox lives in a hole called a den. It usually hunts at night for birds and small mammals.

Sandpiper
The sandpiper is a bird that flies low over the water with short wing beats. It has a shrill, piping call.

FRESHWATER FOREST
pages 12–13

Alligator
Alligators use their snouts and tails to dig holes in the mud, where they lie and keep cool.

Alligator snapping turtle
This turtle uses its wriggling, wormlike tongue as a lure to catch fish.

Anhinga
The anhinga swims with its head and curved neck raised out of the water, looking like a snake.

Brown pelican
This pelican dives head first into water in search of food. It scoops up fish in the pouch under its beak.

Cottonmouth
The cottonmouth is a water snake. It kills small animals with its poisonous fangs.

Eastern coral snake
This colorful snake has bands of red, yellow, and black, which warn other animals that it is dangerous.

Florida panther
The Florida panther is related to the mountain lion, or puma. It lives only in the Everglades.

Garpike
The garpike has thick, armored scales and a very long jaw with many sharp teeth.

Green anole
Anoles are lizards that live mainly in trees and bushes, hunting for insects and small frogs.

Limpkin
The limpkin gets its name from its strange, limping walk. It has broad feet and can move easily on mud.

Manatee
Manatees have paddle-shaped front legs and strong tails that help push them through the water.

Mosquito fish
The small mosquito fish eats its own weight in mosquito larvae each day.

Muskrat
The muskrat eats water plants, such as rushes and cattails, as well as crayfish and snails.

Opossum
When an opossum is in danger, it lies completely still and pretends to be dead.

Purple gallinule
The purple gallinule's long toes spread its weight when walking on lily pads.

Raccoon
Raccoons have thick fur, long bushy tails, and sharp claws that help them climb trees.

Roseate spoonbill
The roseate spoonbill's beak is flat and spoon-shaped. The bird uses it to scoop small animals from the water.

Snail kite
This bird lives only in the Everglades and its only food is the apple snail.

Tree frog
Tree frogs spend most of their time in trees and bushes, which they climb using pads on their feet.

Tree snail
A tree snail can survive long periods of dry weather by sealing all the openings in its shell.

White pelican
White pelicans do not like to perch in trees. They build their nests of stones and sticks on the ground.

Zebra butterfly
The zebra butterfly has larvae that feed on the passion flower.

TUNDRA MAZE
pages 14–15

Arctic fox
The Arctic fox has fur linings on the soles of its feet that help keep it warm in winter.

Arctic hare
The Arctic hare digs burrows in the snow to find vegetation in winter and to provide shelter from the freezing winds.

Arctic skua
Arctic skuas live near other bird colonies so that they can chase the birds and steal their food.

Caribou
Caribou travel together in large herds. They spend the summer on the tundra and the winter in the southern forests.

Dunlin
Dunlins make their nests on the ground. Both male and female share the task of sitting on the eggs.

Fritillary butterfly
The fritillary group of butterflies is usually found in northern countries.

Greater yellowlegs
The greater yellowlegs wades in shallow water, sweeping its bill from side to side to catch small fish, insects, and worms.

Lemming
The lemming grows extra claws on its front legs in the autumn to help it dig. It sheds them in the spring.

Mosquito
A mosquito has two huge eyes, and two antennae that it uses for smelling.

Musk ox
Musk oxen gather into a circle when threatened. Each ox faces outward, with its curved horns at the ready.

Semi-palmated plover
This plover migrates over great distances from the Arctic, flying as far as the southern coasts of South America.

Short-tailed weasel
The short-tailed weasel is small but very strong. It can overpower larger animals, such as rabbits and hares.

Snow goose
Snow geese live in colonies. When they mate, geese stay together for life.

Snowy owl
The snowy owl has thick feathers that cover nearly every part of its body, including the legs and toes.

Tundra redback vole
The redback vole of the tundra spends the winter under the snow, where it keeps warm and can dig for grasses and root bulbs.

Tundra swan
The tundra swan uses its long neck and flat beak to feed on underwater plants.

Willow ptarmigan
Willow ptarmigans eat the shoots of the low-growing dwarf willow and scratch the soil in search of seeds and insects.

Wolverine
A wolverine is not a wolf but a very large kind of weasel. It is fierce and strong and may even attack a young caribou when hungry.

SPOT THE DIFFERENCE pages 16–17

Barasingha
Barasingha, or swamp deer, live in large groups. They have wide, splayed hooves that help them walk on soft ground.

Cattle egret
Cattle egrets nest together in flocks. There may be as many as a hundred egret nests in a single tree.

Gaur
The gaur, or Indian bison, spends the day in the shelter of the trees and comes to the swamp at dusk and dawn to feed.

Hill mynah
The hill mynah is a small dark bird with a noisy range of songs. It nests in holes in trees.

Indian darter
Indian darters are fish-eating birds. Their bills, shaped like daggers, are used for stabbing fish.

Indian elephant
The Indian elephant is smaller than the African elephant. Only the male has tusks.

One-horned rhinoceros
The one-horned rhinoceros has a thick, almost hairless hide that is folded into large plates.

Painted stork
The painted stork is a long-legged wading bird. It has long, broad wings and flies with its neck stretched out.

Pallas's fish-eagle
Pallas's fish-eagle hunts for fish when hungry. It also attacks small water birds and steals food from other animals.

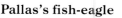

Pheasant-tailed jacana
The pheasant-tailed jacana is a large marsh bird that builds a floating nest on water. Its large toes help it to walk over lilies.

Tiger
Tigers often hunt in marshy areas. They can swim well and stalk their prey through the reeds and undergrowth.

Tiger butterfly
The tiger butterfly contains a poisonous fluid that stops birds and other enemies from eating it.

Tree pie
Tree pies perch on the backs of grazing animals and feed on the ticks that live in the skins.

White-winged duck
The white-winged duck makes its nest in a tree. It is a shy bird, whose black and white feathers make an ideal camouflage.

MYSTERIOUS SALT MARSH pages 18–19

American coot
The American coot lays its eggs in a floating nest built from sticks and water-plant stems.

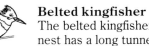

Belted kingfisher
The belted kingfisher digs its nest in the bank. The nest has a long tunnel with a chamber at the end.

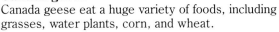

Canada goose
Canada geese eat a huge variety of foods, including grasses, water plants, corn, and wheat.

Clapper rail
This rail gets its name from the rattling sound of its call, which can be heard all over the salt marsh.

Diamondback terrapin
The diamondback terrapin is a turtle, so named because of the diamond-shaped pattern on its shell.

European shrew
The European shrew eats large amounts of food — insects, seeds, and earthworms — during the day.

Glossy ibis
Glossy ibises feed by day in shallow water and fields and roost together at night in waterside trees.

Marsh periwinkle
The marsh periwinkle eats algae. Its droppings help provide nutrients for cordgrass to grow.

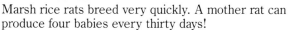

Marsh rabbit
The marsh rabbit uses its strong hind legs to hop across the ground or swim through the water.

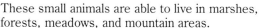

Marsh rice rat
Marsh rice rats breed very quickly. A mother rat can produce four babies every thirty days!

Masked shrew
These small animals are able to live in marshes, forests, meadows, and mountain areas.

Mink
Minks have a warm inner layer of fur and an oily outer layer that keeps them dry when they swim.

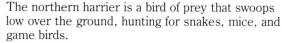

Mosquito
Mosquitoes lay their eggs on or near the water. Without water, the eggs cannot hatch.

Northern harrier
The northern harrier is a bird of prey that swoops low over the ground, hunting for snakes, mice, and game birds.

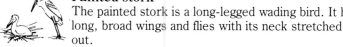
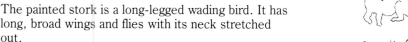

Northern short-tailed shrew
This shrew is the only venomous mammal in North America. It uses its venom, or poison, to kill mice, fish, and newts.

Raccoon
In marshy areas where there are no trees, raccoons nest in tall grasses.

Red-breasted merganser
The red-breasted merganser has a long, hooked bill with a saw-edge that helps the bird grip slippery fish.

Short-eared owl
The short-eared owl often hunts by day. It builds its nest on the ground and warns off intruders with a shrill call.

Short-horned grasshopper
The male grasshopper makes a chirping sound by rubbing his hind legs against a vein on his front wings.

Willet
The willet is a large shore bird. When it is flying, it displays vivid black and white markings on its wings.

Yellow-crowned night heron
These herons feed mainly at night. They wade slowly and silently in shallow water, searching for crabs and fish.

MUDDY MANGROVE

pages 20–21

Black and white tiger butterfly
The black and white tiger butterfly feeds on only one kind of vine, which grows in mangrove swamps.

Black flying fox
The black flying fox is a bat that feeds at night on the flowers of the swamp trees.

Brahminy kite
The brahminy kite eats insects, frogs, and fish. It often builds its nest in mangrove branches.

Brown tree snake
The brown tree snake is agile and dull-colored. It slides along tree branches hunting for small birds to eat.

Carpet python
The carpet python is not poisonous. It kills by wrapping its body around an animal, squeezing it to death.

Cicada
The cicada is found mostly in tropical areas. It feeds on the sap of plants and trees.

Collared kingfisher
This large kingfisher makes its nest in hollow trees, termite mounds, or earth banks.

Fiddler crab
The male fiddler crab has a huge front claw, which it uses for fighting other males and waves to attract females.

Golden orb weaver spider
Orb weaver spiders make round, silken webs between tree branches or flower stems to catch flying insects to eat.

Jabiru
The jabiru has a big, thick bill that it uses to probe the swamp waters for fish and shellfish.

Lilac-crowned wren
The lilac-crowned wren builds a domed nest with a landing platform and an entrance at the side.

Little egret
The little egret feeds on insects and larvae, small fish, crabs, and worms. It makes its nest in trees and bushes.

Longhorn beetle
The longhorn beetle lays its eggs on plant stems. The young may take as long as 3 years to develop into adults.

Mudskipper
The mudskipper is a fish that can travel on land. It pulls itself along with its front fins.

Oyster
An oyster is a shellfish with a soft body inside two hinged shells. Oysters live on the bottom of shallow seas.

Palm cockatoo
The palm cockatoo has a large crest and a curved beak that is strong enough to crack open hard nuts.

Radjah shelduck
The radjah shelduck roosts by day and comes out at night to feed on small water animals and plants.

Saltwater crocodile
The saltwater crocodile is one of the biggest of all crocodiles, growing up to 22 feet in length.

Snake-necked swamp turtle
This turtle has a neck almost as long as its shell. This enables it to hold its head above water while swimming.

Tree frog
The tree frog has long arms and legs, with discs on the toes and fingers. These help it climb trees and reeds.

Weaver ant
The young weaver ants, or larvae, produce a sticky silk that is used to bind the nest together.